Bread for the Winter Birds

By the same author

Poems
The Outer Darkness
The Holy Stone
In the Fire
The Next World
A Smell of Burning
A Breathing Space
The Fourth Man
Selected Poems

Drama
The Judas Tree

Fiction
The Feast of the Wolf

Autobiography
A Clip of Steel

Criticism
The Price of an Eye
Robert Browning

Bread for the Winter Birds

The Last Poems of
Thomas Blackburn

Hutchinson
London Melbourne Sydney Auckland Johannesburg

Hutchinson & Co. (Publishers) Ltd
An imprint of the Hutchinson Publishing Group
3 Fitzroy Square, London W1P 6JD

Hutchinson Group (Australia) Pty Ltd
30–32 Cremorne Street, Richmond South, Victoria 3121
PO Box 151, Broadway, New South Wales 2007

Hutchinson Group (NZ) Ltd
32–34 View Road, PO Box 40-086, Glenfield, Auckland 10

Hutchinson Group (SA) (Pty) Ltd
PO Box 237, Bergvlei 2012, South Africa

First published 1980

© The Estate of Thomas Blackburn 1980

Thanks are due to John Cumming for his help in the preparation of this volume and to *The Tablet* in which some of the poems first appeared

Set in Monotype Bembo

Printed in Great Britain by The Anchor Press Ltd
and bound by Wm Brendon & Son Ltd
both of Tiptree, Essex

British Library Cataloguing in Publication Data

Blackburn, Thomas
   Bread for the winter birds.
   I. Title
   821'. 9'14   PR6003.L26B
ISBN 0 09 143080 1

Contents

Foreword by Peggy Blackburn   7

When   11
Jubilate   12
Alcohol   13
At Dawn   15
Mental Ward   16
Sickness   18
The Hunt   20
Storm   21
I always felt...   22
Rag and Bone   23
To Brynhyfryd   24
Wanting   25
Pain   26
End of a January   27
February   28
Cold   29
April   31
Becomings   32
The Magdalene   33
Pax   34
Serenity   35
I put aside the anxiety and the fear...   36
William Wordsworth   37
Ash-Tree   39
Zennor   41
Nearing the Summit   42
Metaphoric   43
The Authorized Version   44
Dormire   45
Laudate   47
Blackbird   48
Swallows   49

Gulls   50
The Silences   51
Bread for the Winter Birds   52
Crag of Craving   53
Aquarius   54
Winter Solstice (1)   55
Winter Solstice (2)   56
Revenants   58
Morituri   60
Posthumous   61
As I Am Known   62
Venite   63
Logos   64
In Memoriam: Kevin   65
Rain After Drought (Maundy Thursday)   67
Growing Pains   68
Speed, Speed   69
Gerard Manley Hopkins   70

Foreword

Several of the poems in this collection were written during the last few days of Thomas's life, and I feel the need to tell something about those days.

Our coming to Wales had never been more glorious. The colours along the road had an almost supernatural beauty. When we were still twenty miles from our destination all the veils appeared to be lifted, and we could see beyond our mountain Cnicht – the sleeping Knight – to the sweep and grandeur of the Snowdon range. Thomas was silent; he knew and loved these mountains so well. Often on our journeys to Wales in the recent past his face would darken and become sombre as we neared his old climbing grounds. But on this, the last journey, his spirit seemed to be free of all painful regret.

We reached the cottage while the summer evening was still bright. The little house was welcoming, but there was none the less a strange atmosphere, hidden and brooding. I wished that I could have had one of the children with me to share the beauty of the blue evening, and to help dispel my curious sense of desolation. I could not reach Thomas; he appeared heavy and animal, remote and intense.

Our first day was spent with friends, and Thomas promised that he would take them for a long walk, to the deserted village at the head of the valley perhaps, or over the ridge of Cnicht. He never fulfilled his promise; it was as if he could not for a moment pause from his writing: letters, letters, poems, and the last chapter of an autobiographical work, which now had, he declared, a happy ending.

The next day we went to a friend's exhibition of paintings and afterwards sat by the seashore near Harlech Castle. Thomas didn't even look towards the sea or at his beloved sea birds; he sat on a sand dune amongst the lavender and the marram grasses, oblivious of me and of everything around him. We stayed there for nearly an hour, and I have that vivid memory of the brightness of the sea, the scent of herbs, the ragged golden walls of the castle basking like an old lion in the sun, and the silent strange presence of a living man who was not with me at all.

On the fourth day Thomas asked me if the birds flying down by the river bank were swallows, and I was surprised because he knew the flight and shape of birds so well.

On the fifth day he wrote the serene and delicate poem 'Morituri'. It was soon to be read at his own graveside, by the poet R. S. Thomas who came from his parish at Aberdaron to utter a last blessing.

On the last day no visitors came. My brother had left, and I was conscious of his absence. I watched Thomas anxiously. He was very preoccupied, and carried his blue manuscript book with him wherever he went – going out for short walks, calling next door to ask the neighbours for something. In his restlessness he was avoiding being alone, or alone with me. He did read me the 'Morituri' poem, and then briefly I felt happier, as if for a moment a different air had breathed on us and the bitter cup had passed from us. But it was only momentary, and he said he must work again, perhaps through the night, and I was not to worry. My depression returned, and I went to bed and tried to read myself into enough quiet to fall asleep.

Thomas came to say goodnight. He kissed me gently and lovingly and yet somehow in a perfunctory manner. He had the blue exercise book under his arm. I remember him bending his head to go out of the low door: the light on the yellow silk bedcover, the night sounds of mosquitoes and owls and the whispering of the ash-trees.

I waited among those night sounds. I dozed a little and fell into a half-dream. At about two or three in the morning there was a terrible cry. My first reaction was that he must have gone out of his mind and I was saturated with fear. I came out of my room. I remember thinking that the door to that room was matchwood and I was without any protection. Then there came the tearing sound of the body's death and I knew that the spirit had already gone, it had fled with the cry. I found him on the floor between the dark window and the bed, a massive staring shape, the eyes pale. May God have mercy on us, for all eternity, de profundis. I held on to that heavy hand and let it grow cold in mine. My thoughts were disordered, and I felt a sharp pain of pity for us both. Loneliness, anguish and the awful still fear that death brings.

I lit a candle, covered him with a faded Indian rug, and sat beside him on the floor waiting for the daylight. The colours of the rug were beautiful, like a benediction. Then day began to dawn and, with the rose light coming up from behind the mountains, the candle flame grew pale. The world seemed a strange and empty place.

Before coming to bed, Thomas had been writing a long letter to his brother. At one point in it he said, 'It seems what was meant to be a poem and a short but loving letter has turned into a long essay, and I will type out two copies in the morning.' In this letter he gave his own account of those last days:

. . . I went to bed quite early last night but woke up at six to the dawn and the sea birds. I wrote from seven a.m. to six p.m., and completely changed the final chapter of my autobiography. Only now have I reached the serenity I had not then attained; I had fobbed off the solution with a clatter of futile euphemisms.

. . . Six-fifteen. Undrugged but unskinned by three months of abstinence from alcohol that to me was poison. I watch the sea birds drift as if nerved by a single hand, as they do every first light. A single magpie lighted on a fence two or three yards from my typewriter and I thought one for sorrow, and pulled my forelock, but another came and it was mirth, and the two brisking about in the rinsed light all gold and glory. Then a third came and it was the funeral of sorrow and mirth in the tragic joy of all opposition that includes but exceeds understanding.

. . . A good August and a beautiful morning.

. . . Ten o'clock, and though I have worked through three-quarters of the night I feel no tiredness. Peggy, though she slept from half-past ten through to ten a.m., is bitterly cross about my unslept bed. It is strange; well she must just get used to a relatively longer-timetabled creature who, provided it is unpilled, can sleep when it pleases.

. . . Ten o'clock, no, ten-thirty. In the present of at last learning to love. Peace, breakfast, a walk, talk, sleep, and humility, humility is endless.

. . . I have talked with my selfness, the godhead of my birth. It seemed that my father Eliel and my mother Adelaide – though my hair prickled at the prospect – were here. Recently I have in dreams met again the godhead, and going I recalled coming. I have heard the godhead speak as he spoke at first, desiring to be born into that by no means easy conjunction of Blackburn and Fenwick. 'So,' said the voice, 'you have indeed come through. I thought at times it might be intolerable, but now you have grown into the Thou of the Intention. Now you will grow here. No more will you need the iron maiden of carnality. Dear child, I have worked with you, and you will grow here where the eternals are to further dyings and births, here in the dominion of the spirit.'

> Thou hast delivered my soul from birth
> My darling from the power of the dog
> Natal finite
> Finite natal
> Peace, peace, peace.

... I have relived on the page the frightening and complete blackness. I was led, supported by the Virgilian guide, beneath the hairy scrotum of the King of Darkness, to rock, wan light, sun light, gloria.

... Now after hours of strange travel from dawn to dawn, though the mind still burns, I must lie in a horizontal position and breathe long and deep.

When

What terror, what sudden dread;
A mad man wakes in his straw;
Cold, sweating, upright in bed,
A child wakes and watches his door,
As from his cellarage
A mad man climbs up a stair.

But the lunatic cannot come in
To the room of the haunted child.
O, when will it come about,
Eyes skinned so he understand,
That a child, upright, unafraid,
Take a blind, mad man by the hand?

Jubilate

When it finally comes may we rejoice,
If it should happen and it will happen – I hope I do not go before.
I hope so because my pension will stop when I die,
But about the actual dying we could be happy
For it is a particular and specific grace.

We go into a novel and beatific freedom
Of being without the darkened glass
And into the spirit where there is no touch, kingdom
Of a singular intensity of the being that really is.

An interchange without any mask of rectitude
Where since lying and touch do not exist there
Those for whom crime is habit where there is no crime
Wait by the river of weeping to return further.

I am sure I will be with you in that area
Of being with those we love and sympathetic strangers,
And that you will continue to paint and I to write poetry
On a medium where no canvas is needed or paper,
Since thought and image there are engraved reality
And all creation is what that dimension does foster
In a particular verity of identity.

Alcohol

Why in each whispering
Gap of the minute
So much of torsion
To be diluted,
Like scrubbing out words in
A concern for blankness
As if non-being
Felt for my throat for
Desires of dying.
But just once more, once. . . .
A valid coinage
Is in my later age
What should be long since
Whitened from the page.
I mean that another
Dosage of blankness
May nourish Sadness
To such a point that
Hope becomes hopeless
And from delirium
No way of returning.
It's a question of being
Aware every moment
Of rationalizations for
The slow killing intent
Not to feel or suffer,
To bypass new growing
By having nothing to offer.
I shall be a person
Who, more than opiates, is
Open to each season's
Intensities,
Listen to each occasion,
The wolf leader's cry

For murder, self-murder,
'Tomorrow he'll die.'
That my next day may not be an infernal
Uncurtaining of sorrow
But, rain rinsed eternal,
The cavorting creature,
Pliable as water,
But in every feature
Firm set as granite,
Bronzed by the new light
Of any good morning,
Fashioned for delight,
Adorned and adorning.

At Dawn

Have you ever had moments when the curtain lifted
And showed you deeper ways of how to see,
As if away the mist on creatures drifted
And fixed them with a new intensity?

I find it when I work on till the morning
And, just before dawn breaks, chorals of birds
Fracture the greyness with great peals of singing,
No frost or drifting rain ever retards.

I walk into the street with my old dog then
Watching the plane-trees slowly taking shape
As if on the first day of a lost Eden,
And its novelty is similar to hope,

Which isn't really something that you wish for,
Like a new watch or car or even a friend,
But just sereneness which when it does occur
Cancels words out like 'beginning' or an 'end'.

One morning just near dawn I heard the sound
Of an arrowhead of water-seeking swans
Beating up, no doubt, to the twin lakes of Richmond
From the muddier reaches of their native Thames.

Whiter than dawn they were, but such a seeing
On such a novelty of singing day
Seemed in its felicity of being
To hint at words I haven't learnt to say.

Mental Ward

I recall the hygienic wards,
The needle pressed to my arm
To avert me from alcohol,
The intolerable, restless pain
Of those who are sick at heart,
And surfacing out of sleep,
New day's antiseptic dirt.
I knew time passes by,
As wan hope and sole comfort,
That no moment's eternity,
In that chartered space I did know
How far out in the ranging sea,
He shoots bird, fish and seal,
The master of the arrow.

I am measured every day,
Blood, water, brain and pulse,
And sick, remembering myself,
Feel I've become someone else,
A delinquent nonentity
Nurse, doctors work upon.
Today it is ECT
And God knows how the colours run
From a world I used to know,
Though he straddles the far-off sea
The master of the arrow.

We take our medicine
At regular intervals
In a queue of origin,
Wait for it to mollify
Those claws that tear at the heart;
The move of good life, again,
Will it never, never start?

Lost men and women stare
On blankness with cold, dead eyes,
Lost in a world drained dry
Or of menacing fantasies.
Will I leave this? I cannot know,
But, master of ringing seas,
Make me the shaft of your bow.

Sickness

It is not a question of anguish
Or even anxiety,
The fact that upstairs you languish
In pale humidity,
But of brooding over the letters
Of a book I cannot read
Since those who know its language
Are silent because they are dead.

In your bedroom I hear you coughing
Like the preface to a page
Of the book of those who if living
Do so beyond the siege
Of our zest by a temporal body
And the clock of a beating heart:
I sit in my book-lined study
With my old dog, under your hurt.

But no book on the shelves about me
Gives light to the one on my knees
Whose pages are made out of nothing,
Its letters silences,
Though the white of the growing morning
And you still after violences
Of retching and of coughing,
Suggests by the shaping trees
A species of understanding
Between the living and dead,
As if this day was an image
Of what can't be written or said.

I know you too well to forget you
Can rise reborn from the sea
Of your lungs or a temporal anguish

Like that queen, and suddenly
Put on life like a new dress,
And do not think when you waken
As I stand to watch you asleep
Any golden bowl will be broken,
So firm the compact you keep
With a potency of breathing.
So I think about growing pains
And will not ring up the doctor.
These trees and this grass are they signs
Of what we are growing for?
The silence of morning is fractured
And the postman knocks at the door.

The Hunt

You were sad this evening; then you began to speak
Of my obvious shortcomings and passionately,
And I did not interrupt the tale you hammered out,
Knowing that to be its theme was called for from me.

So you said, with emphasis, that I was plain nasty
And I agreed since I do not want to be 'nice',
Nor did I mind when you said I ate the dog's biscuits and was greedy,
And that you couldn't bear the 'holier than thou' look on my face;

After all one is human and not some evangelical,
Unimpassioned, unconflicting inhabitant of nowhere,
And although of your grief and rage I was willing to take all,
I felt no shame, not even a sense of pressure.

For I divined what pristine hate and sorrow were under
The strain of your heart and torsion of your head,
And that unleashing the war dogs meant sanity,
But I guessed, as you did, Poseidon's dogs would not tear me
Or you would not have released them with such freedom;
I mean that I have claimed as my own their savagery
After racing with the pack in the red kingdom.

It was good last night watching you watch your unloosed dogs of fury
And you look stronger today since rage is no more an enemy.
Now that you have broken down the kennel bars
The great beasts stalk serene through your heart and house in Putney,
We will sleep tonight under a few ungrieving stars.

Storm

What a blind night,
I mean both with rain and wind
And what is equally great
The storm in the heart and mind
At having, approaching sixty,
Raged at my most best loved,
Like a drunken psychopath,
Beat, grabbed and crushed and raved
In an ecstasy of wrath,
Wishing but to obliterate.
Must the obverse of the coin, love,
Be stamped with such image of hate?
I call down this bitter season
Of a germed and blind November,
Bear witness to the passion
With which this night I remember
A madman, a woman, a child,
And the witherings of anger.

I always felt . . .

I always felt that with the next drink I would see God
But it was never true; what I got was a hangover,
A melancholia that was incomparably sad,
And then drink again the ruinations to cover.
Now after an orgy of sparkling wine
I have been dry for ten days, a long time for me,
And enjoy the sense of well being not drinking
And enduring neat the melancholy,
Like not retreating when the waters boom and rave
But sitting on a near rock bearing them accurately
And feeling their bitter spray on my face and hands
And then walking to my bedroom,
Not visiting on the way the nearest bar,
But knowing, even if I do not sleep, morning will lift the gloom
Which thrives on retreating from things as they are.
But there is no such word as stasis,
You can go forward or you can go back
And going back is contracting the spaces,
Holding a novel bottle by the neck,
Till you are one whose God is the off-licence,
Consummation going home with four bottles in a bag,
Ready to commit a brimming violence
As you empty a full tumbler at one swig,
Pulling the curtains down so people will not see you,
Knocking the bottles back in the hope that you
Will gain freedom for the next drink or the next one
And finding yourself in time like a sticky glue,
The soul and spirit bulging out like an abuse
Of whatever they are destined to go through,
But bypass by drinking till you are shaking
And paranoid vision is all that is left for you.
But in a week it will be my sixty-first birthday
It is time I came to terms with my sorrow,
So goodnight grief and good morning tomorrow.

Rag and Bone

Poetry, said Yeats, comes from quarrels in the mind
And that poetry is not compatible with being at peace,
Yet it is tranquillity that I hope to find
And the search for that and the poems need not cease.

Surely if one reaches the self and the ego dies,
Then further reaches of saying are in potential being,
Alien to the obsession that moans and raves,
Further deeper areas of speaking and seeking.

Poems indeed but without the hurt
Implicit always in the unfractured circle of selfness
Outside, 'The foul rag-and-bone shop of the heart,'
Speaking of the energies that exceed mere stress.

'De profundis clamo ad te Domine.'
Since the request has been made and the answer given
We speak no more with a marred identity,
But with the syllables appropriate to heaven.

To Brynhyfryd

Again back to the cottage where I
Seldom wish to go anywhere else except to the quiet of Putney,
I expect stars unskinned from the pink fuss of the city
And the stream turning its stones under the dark mountain,
The paths to houses where friends sit by the fire and maintain
By simply being themselves enough interest to sustain
The time from eight till midnight.
It is the quiet of the dark people illuminates
A presence each definition underrates,
To so much more than the word relates,
I mean presences, behind presences, behind presences
Exceed the diagnosis of the five senses
And fill more than a room with their unpunctuatable sentences.
It is merely lifting a hand that penetrates through
All it is possible for the pronouns to say;
What enormous gestures when you speak to me or I to you.
It is the words behind the words that are said
Which are subterfuges by which those anciently or just dead
Find a means by which what they did not understand is interpreted,
So that rereleased in this room by the word, the word
Helps those whose dying was complicated or came hard;
Alive in her death, my mother is glad my pages occurred.
And style is making words to be heard both here and there
In an arrangement which few acknowledge now but many dead
   hear;
To the human breath it brings the Immortals near,
And does not vapour away like casual speech on the wind,
Being hard, well, what is hardest here, as a diamond,
Style in speech which after death does not end,
Trapping, as it does, the mystery of a man, of a woman,
In their forms both human, and dead and inhuman,
It is the bird which sings for joy after acute pain.

Wanting

Whatever the wanting is, the want's available
If sincerely wanted as I wanted to be
Free of the stranglehold of alcohol,
And like winter lightning I found myself and was free.

After the metaphors of agony
Into the eternals where the eternals are
And I grip with a firm hand and with clear eyes see,
The wanting is the praying and the power.

Never again will I drink; that I know
Having sweated it out silently without euphemisms
A terrible cacophony of drums
Upon my flesh blow after crippling blow,

Sensing the reality of what I was
In a strange poise between hell and heaven
Where at last the dice were quite uneven,
Loaded against, drinking forever is.

It's gone now and I know what is here,
I am with the glories where the glories are
After travelling through so many corridors and cells
And crawling under Satan's genitals,
I saw the benediction of a star.

Pain

If the pain were not bearable
It would not be given us to bear;
At finding excuses not to bear pain I am too plausible,
Trying to dissipate the angst by chemicals into warm air.

Some degree of pain is synonymous with growing,
The real anguish is in the running
From what is ourselves and close as our own breathing;
Take pain into heart and mind and it becomes tolerable,
There is even joy in our becoming more mature.

Pain is woven into our workings here
And will continue to remain so until
You and I with the immortals are
On the other side of the hill.

End of a January

Two, green and white when the cold is
At the extremity of the heartache of winter,
But there they are and their coloured promises
From this rime speaking, from the heart's centre.

Snow dropping tonight on the snowdrop's petals
Out in the dark where the puffed birds are;
Still it is spring, and the old story tells
Of gold fuses on their green stalks moving together.

White and green they are, a vegetable counterpart
Of the snowdrops of the spirit we shall all inherit,
For they are in the archetypes of the heart
And that is what all the breathing and the bother is about.

More vivid there than here the colours are
Who rely now on the five blurred senses,
In their being beyond where only the carnals occur
In a forever ongrowing of forever Easter.

February

New in their attitudes of grace and light
The snowdrops and the golden celandine
Speak words I almost am able to interpret,
Changing with the fitful sunshine and the rain,
And there's a kind of going forward now
It's February, a silent whispering;
Is it those minute buds on the ash-tree bough?
Never was I so aware of the year's changing.
It's emphasized by myself who also am moving
After a decade of stasis though I don't know,
Despite the fact I've waited very long,
Just where it is that life intends me to go,
Except that it will be a movement and a stillness
Like the swift impetus of a mountain stream
Which though it bubbles on to greater waters
Keeps its exact shape and contours all the same.
I mean moving to death there's no need to
Lose hold on my special individuality
Or lament the final promontories I pass through
Since 'not being' isn't in my vocabulary.
Those green shoots latent in the spring-time garden
Come March – will unfold into the daffodil,
And so we will expect out of our latent person
Novel patterns of colour, ripeness is all.

Cold

How cold this eve of March is,
The wind like a honed sword
Penetrating what clothes us,
Now there's no morning bird
To start the dawn chorus
Thoughts dwindle in the cold
When one is walking
Huddled in overcoats,
Feeling, not thinking.

At home where it is warm
I think of awareness,
What lies where escape or storm
Its complicated start has,
Think in immediate instance
Of what here and now is
And probe each circumstance
To its hidden causes.

Crocuses, snowdrops,
Above the sharp soil are,
Above the chill steps
Of this bad weather;
I am by degrees
Bringing events together
To their original
Of turpitude, confusion,
Into the light of day
Its illumination.

The plants of spring their
Strong energies fashion
Out of cool tomts of seed
In brilliant colours
Living from dying,
Rightness from errors,
Novelties of seeing.

April

Strange I will not see the mountains for three months and a little more
Since like January this Easter very cold is, very raw,
And it will be like wet ice in our cottage in Croesor,
Dampness seeping through and congealing on the grey slates of the floor
And the Welsh wind creeping through the windows and inaccurate door.
But it seems to see no buzzard, ravens, sheep – I do not care,
Since within my heart and my mind they are present evermore.
With me on this April morning though they are not present here
In my being, near dawn, brooding, they could not be much closer,
Buzzard, curlew, raven, heron, in my mind's eye they are here.
And those mountains Cnicht, Moelwinian, could not be a jot nearer,
Perhaps it's because last zero summer, no walking, a cracked lumbar,
So I sat in the great heat taking in the fells' fauna.
Gleaning into my mind each detail, mountain bracken and heather,
So that now they are co-present where the streets of London are;
My forever salient Alpha and eternal Omega.

Becomings

Living, and with some success, the man I am supposed to be,
And having rumbled how many odorous sideways, vagrant
 pressure,
Perhaps I am at long last on the line intended for me,
Not that it is easy, why should it be?
The moping deathsheads and everywhere the phantasma
Sidling up with its 'I am, I am you, be in me.'
But there's no doubt, how could one accept the offer
And settle down to a limited, static solidity?
Impossible after having known spaciousness.
Not that it's easy to keep to the unfolding path
Whose guiding line does not spin out automatically,
One treads the way and is neither stopped by neurotic or
 psychopath,
It is helping to create the zest that is creating me.

The Magdalene

Because she loved much, she is much beloved
And what the dear lord said
On our pulses shall be proved,
When we lie awake in the dark,
Racked, sweating and unclean,
The saint we turn to for comfort
Is Mary Magdalene.

She was the first to see
The risen body of a God,
Red roses they grow best from
A sanguine vesture of mud.
When your hand shakes in the morning
And you don't know where you have been,
Take the harlot for your comfort:
Saint Mary Magdalene.

She poured the precious ointment
On the feet of the condemned Christ;
He too had gone through those sins
And the sharp attritions of lust,
Otherwise he would not be human.
Those who sweat and tremble
And can't end, since they can't begin,
Silent, blue lady remember,
Saint Mary Magdalene.

One need not, of course, make her journey
(I haven't been to the Himavant),
Certain things come well enough from hearsay,
Sex should be a sacrament.
But when the people and landscape shrivel
Into pain and it is obscene,
She may well be of relevance,
Our Lady Magdalene.

Pax

It is only now in my sixth decade that, instead of
Trying to live life, I let life live me;
Why it should do so and so belatedly?
I'm not sure though it has something to do with love.
What I mean to say is enjoying myself and others by no half
Measure but by letting life be and be through me,
Using my energies for what is destiny, the creature
Is loved by its friend and creator. I baulked
Until now ramming into shapes the pattern of my being
I lived a parody; it was sex, rocks, alcohol,
I did not know, though depressive, the latter is a depressant
And made all but the hepped-up instant intolerably dull,
Or that one must be aware of being instant by instant.

I am, as Blake said, the secretary of the word
And to get words down with an extreme accuracy
Have ravaged myself almost to excess and with brutality.
Lighten our darkness for we tend to live in the half-dark.
Growing to live in poetry, the poetry at last wafts home to my
  neighbour.
I mean what I wrote with the writing the only reward.

Serenity

Where have you come from, you strange visitor
After the riot, confusion and distress,
Outbreathing syllables of charity and peace,
The pilot of the soul, the avatar?

It's two a.m., the dawn I'd like to come through,
The starless swaddled kingdom of the word
Before the chorus, hear the pristine bird
Dragging the images out into first view.

I'm sixty-one, after decades of confusion
Serenity settled down upon my shoulders
Like the ravens of that god verity whispers
And at last the syllables know how to scan.

Never did I think I would be enjoying
Limited conversation and for its own sake,
But sit and listen and sometimes wide awake
The small talk will glisten into steadfast burning.

No more the senses are drenched with alcohol
That depressive that after a short jag
Makes the scarified instances sink and sag,
The soaked cells of the brain clammy and dull.

It's strange to find serenity at sixty-one
After so many decades that were infernal.
Ah well, as Lear has said, 'Ripeness is all.'
I'd like a little time, though, not to be Legion.

And to enjoy serenity and charity
And make poems not quarrelling with myself
But eagle-winged over that swirling gulf,
Before the stern bell tolls out, 'Come with me!'

I put aside the anxiety and the fear . . .

I put aside the anxiety and the fear
And praise the fact that they have gone away,
Unquiet has gone in a simple night and day
And it is peace that is drawing near.
A kind of unclenching of the tumultuous heart
As nearer to coming on I slowly come,
To the silence after the viaticum
And sensing the whole of things within a part.

Serene, no more Medusa's serpents hiss
And the emptied ego here is rammed full of soul
In a tolerance that is founded and grafted and whole,
The situation is as it really is.
The mind yields metaphors just as it pleases
And with no language talks to anyone who
It wishes to be with and talking to
In a rapportage where communions bless;
I put aside the torment and the fear
And what I was before conditioning draws near.

Which has of course to be interpreted,
And day by day I grow more conscious of where
The merciless, hidden, condemners really are
Within the mindstuff and the ticking heart,
And finding them is where I find my freedom
That myself by night and by the daylight too
Helps me to understand that other called you,
The intricacies of light and dark that come.
I, aside the torment and the fear,
Understand my conditioning in this doomed here.

William Wordsworth

He's hard to understand unless you've had
Some inkling of the lifting that he knew
When presences one tends to link with God
Behind phenomena loomed. Clean through

Stones, brooks and trees, this Cumbrian could see,
Taking its shape and almost speaking words,
Reality behind reality,
Splintering a dayscape into dusty shards.

It's paranormal, no doubt, this faculty,
And unless your senses have once taken leave
Of creatures of mere tangibility,
If one came from the dead you'd not believe.

Dangerous this work of lifting of the veil,
But since strong as the rock his personality
He could speak out where usual words must fail,
And knew such speaking was his destiny.

So he wrote down how 'breathings' haunted him,
A crag stalked after his small, stolen boat,
Shadowing his days with presences and unseen
Powers that were joyful, terrible and part

Of the 'wisdom and spirit of the universe'
And which it was his duty to record –
Lunatics know this well and it's their curse –
But he was wise and did not stretch the cord

Beyond that point where it was sure to break
And with it any sense of men and speech.
He strode the world of dreams when broad awake
And showed how short and dull our usual reach.

The world, he rightly tells us, is most strange,
And suggested how to break such thought
As he narrows the confines of a landscape round us
To the minutiae of a closet's range
And see it as it is, an endlessness.

He spoke of those sacred moments when the burden
Of all this weary world is rolled away
And with it the sour detritus and boredom
Of walking with narrowed eyes convention's way.

Now, since he wrote a fraction nearer to
Its terror and its glory, this limitless world,
He taught us a new way of knowing through
Our numberless senses, more open, less tightly furled.

Ash-Tree

Ash-trees before our cottage,
Yggdrasil, the world tree,
I must forgive my father
If he is to pardon me
For, although he once committed
Abominations countless,
He will know now his errors
And sympathize with my distress,
As I do with the dark colours
Marking his quietus.
For he did not do what is evil,
Though his mistaken good
Was on my hand a stigma
And I coughed up mucus and blood.
He thought that my well being
Depended on his being strong
In his battle contra natura
But could not have been more wrong
And flogged me under a picture
Of the trees of Gethsemane
And loathed the love my mother
Excessively showered on me.
I've revenged myself with a book.
Has he read it where he is?
I doubt if it was a shock
Since the dead transcend detritus
And he may now be forgiving,
Understand the catharsis it was
That forbade my pardoning
As I forgive him now
And so doing have freedom to breathe in
Packing my guilts away,
And novelties of living
Rise like the breaking of day.

In this garden a plethora
Of birds and flowers and a stone
Lion's head that stares through
Miasmas of fantasies
To a central immanence,
And think forgiving is loving
Though little of love is owed
To an old priest of the country;
But I chose him to be bestowed
And no one else for my journey
Down here where the creatures are
And blind eyes learn to see,
Soon in Snowdonia
I will sit beneath the world tree.

Zennor

Where the Carracks are near Zennor
In Bosigran's old Count House
In spite of a fractured lumbar
I would this day of March
Scramble delicately down to
The crinkled metal of the sea,
Potencies of night and day,
Watch the sentinel cormorants
Keeping watch over the bay
And the kittiwakes making their noises
On the steeps of Porthmoina,
Where the shags above the waters
Whiten their small rocky stance
And a seal swings, sated with mackerel
In his marine circumstance,
Looks at you with talking brown eyes
In a kind of seeing dance.
Oystercatchers further over
Probe a narrow stretch of sand,
Red-beaked, black and white uncover
Sea bits under the island,
With the brown and piping dunlin
Feeding with them side by side
Where the shrimps are, little fishes
Stranded at the low of tide.
Enormous cliffs I used to climb once
Now are just to love and view
Not a place up which to advance,
But by eyesight to undo.
I can't have enough of seeing
Or of feeling the sea wind
Near the Count House where a fading
Body nourishes the mind.

Nearing the Summit

Under the telescopic July sun
Each detail of the mountain by my house
Seems what a Chinese master has well done
And what an india-rubber could erase.
Yet climb it and you sweat from stone to grass
And grope and grapple every step of the way,
Each moment growing more steep and strenuous,
You only reach the summit by what you pay.

I used to think that life a pageant was,
But now I know that it is an ordeal
And one must grit one's teeth and make no fuss
As one sweats through the stringencies of what's real.
It's something to do with a pliant kind of zest
That still insists that joyfulness is a fact
Though we've no hiding place or lasting rest
And all immediacies such joys restrict.

Knowing this we extend our space and time
Into a careless medium and more free
And postulate that by death we are taking aim
Into a novel kind of ecstasy.
Maybe this grows as the good muscles soften
And we no longer can enjoy the sweet
Taste of success as all the crag routes harden
And we can't love the airs beneath our feet,
Coming towards the summit it is sterner
And what the good will be there I don't know,
Perhaps it will be easier to ask pardon,
I haven't been there but it may be so.

Metaphoric

Wanlight upon the water,
The last gasp of carmine scree
To marsh where the reeds take over,
Grant me time in which to see
And sense the sense of forever
This lake brings home to me.

So does sweating over that mountain
Called the Cnicht till it runs down
To the grass and heather, sodden,
The soaked turf of the coomb
Which filters down through boulders
To beget the youth of a stream.

Why do we feel nostalgia
When scenes like this strike home?
Is it because we remember
A glory not fixed by time
And towards which our living is travelling?
I think of a metaphor
In the sun that is creeping over
This orison of Easter birds;
It is good to be a lover,
But love always exceeds the words.

The Authorized Version

Remember the words do
Include the silences
And that some words are
Alive in their pauses
The divine can breathe in.
For themes of the spirit
Need gaps to suggest how
No words quite inherit
Themes that supreme are,
So the great words meet
With sound and silence.
They need what is not
Quite said for truth's sake:
And since we're finite
Only the silences
Can suggest infinite
Meetings, humilities.

Dormire

Watching here in the garden
And the colours green or blue,
I am delighted this morning
As I sit and drink tea with you.
Author, originator
Of the flowers which grace this day
In a now and continual present
In which I am learning to be
Mortal in sunshine though recent
In immortality.

To bowls of bread and water
The starling and blackbirds come
And thrushes and sparrows though winter
Has perished; summer's kingdom
Was absolute this May morning,
Sleepless at dawn at first light
I heard them start to sing,
The birds in the trees of the garden,
Their world has no ending.

I knew that summer and winter
Was only a metaphor
Of a state of sleepless being
Dying at last I'll enter.
Now though in seasons occur
Varied states of being human
That to be serene one must let
The eternities sign with a first name
And never ever forget.

The lion's stone head in the garden,
It outstretches time and space,
To live in time, in periods,
Is what I must learn to bless;
Who seek for the grace of forever
And in consequence suffer distress,
Since now is a question of periods
Though posthumous we'll be
Growing and growing forever
In an eternity.

Laudate

There the sea birds come at first light in all weathers, on all days,
To a particular field for feeding, feathered in the sun's faint rays,
And through sleep I still catch their sea cries,
Turning my dreams to ocean themes whose great rhythm never
  dies,
Think of cliffs of sleep till some great hand sends the birds on
  their highways,
Draws them back when it is evening to the coigns above the bays;
Master hand that with a difference on our human being plays
And will never let us fall, for death as an end is a pack of lies,
This the wind that blows at midnight to the stars above us says,
Age is but a growing nearer to being without what flesh purveys
So however bad the weather what is there to do but praise.

Blackbird

Trouser-leg we call the blackbird
Who lives in the pyrocanthus in our garden,
And he sings for joy when the first light has almost occurred.
We put out scraps and water when the black months harden

And as now when it's April and his mate is nesting
In the prickly tree he has made his own,
It is an unspeaking communion but seems lasting
With this bird whose drooping leg-feathers prompted our name,

And when, as happens, I write the night out,
It's his aubade reminds me it's a new day,
Than his crescendo with its last held note
Who could desire more fitting prelude and jubilee?

Even when I mow the lawn, he will walk about pecking
At bits of things despite the clatter
And to see what has been turned up in the mowing.
I like our intimacy. It does matter

More than much ersatz communion
With people who fill up the silence by word after meaningless
    word,
And so break the pauses we grow on,
Then I hold to the yellow bill and shining of our blackbird.

Swallows

The swallows fly at first light
Close to the stones of the lane
For insects in their giddy dawn flight
Are low, for it's chilly again.
But soon under the eaves they'll be building
Their nests from spittle and mud,
As they've done world without end
By a wisdom they have and had.

It is six o'clock in the morning
And I who cannot sleep
Watch these birds returning
And see the dawn taking shape
In trees and flowers and the blue-lit
Flash of a sudden wing,
As if an equation had come right
As it was in the beginning.

I mean that on this June morning
The swallows guided from far
Distances in blood are burning
In a place as particular
As my choice of a place to be born in
Before my birth into life
When the breathing shadows begin,
Though neither welcome or safe,
But the nature of destiny
As the swallows cross the desert
And acres of green sea.

Gulls

The sea birds gather
One hour after daybreak
In the field where the sheep are.
Like a word new lights speak
Then leave by an impulse
For the lake of the mountain;
Next dawn they'll be here again.

Who is it utters their
Planned destined journey
Through the clear and rinsed air,
So to accost me?
If I knew who did
Sign with his signature
Bird, field, and morning,
I should find ever more
Accurate meaning.

As it is they come
Through the cleansed daylight
From the sea's kingdom
Never early or late
To the field by my cottage
Where I've worked through till daybreak,
Uttered and uttering.

The Silences

Silences indivisible are
But there can be silence
That many people share
Companionable;
If to bear solitude
One has learnt to be able
But that attitude
Is inescapable.

I have learnt quiet
By being greatly unstable,
The verities of being undeft
By nursing home, hospital,
Of consciousness bereft
In shock electrical.

Now in my last decades,
On the edge of retirement,
Violence, chaos fades
And I am intent
On what my end hides;
Catch, although at times faint,
That which never fades
But is ever present,
And of turmoil, neap tides
Is the fulfilment.

Bread for the Winter Birds

Very cold the weather is,
The puddles cat-ice,
Frost on the grasses,
For the winter birds no grace
Nor morning choral
In February's stiffness
Freezing and mortal
To the limits of stress.

Sixty-one in eight days
And so much to say still
So many bent ways
To unwind and fulfil,
The mind honing its edge as
Grosser the physical,
Closer to what is
Pristine, eternal.

Do the birds dying
In the mantled hedgerow
Resume their flying
Beyond ice and snow,
Yield to the bright morning's
Sunrising chorus?
There must be birdsinging
In the areas for us;
After the day of doom,
Daffodils, roses,
My spirit takes aim
To scan new pages.

Crag of Craving

Tonight a moon, and a star
Of unusual potency
Break the conventional blur
Of this time-chartered city,
Bringing with them Snowdonia,
My cottage under such sky
And the smell of the mountain night,
Loaded with heather and hay,
Salt water smells from the bright
Disc of Tremadoc Bay.

And it is all waiting there,
Like the other side of a death,
For spring's more clement weather
And then summer; a tapping moth
Outside the window where I sit
Long after embalmed midnight
Seeking the appropriate word
For some wandering soul in limbo
Who does not know death has occurred
But has nowhere but dying to go.

I think of the twin lakes under
The Crag of Craving and their
Uncompromised gesture of splendour,
Their water lapping on scree,
And the sense it gives of some other
Uncircumscribed quality,
To which you and I will come;
It's beyond the Crag of Craving
But I cannot give it a name.

Aquarius

How long now since the golden
Zest of the moment wholly possessed me?
Climbing gave it, scaling some rock face,
'La sua voluntate', it was my peace.
I'd feel as each page of granite turned over
The joy of the moment that is forever;
But climbing, stalling at about forty,
Became what I did from a sense of duty,
The clouded space which toe and forefinger
Had scaled with delight, a nuisance, a danger;
So forsaking the great worlds of the climber,
Brooding on lake and tor, I became a walker.

The zest of the moment love gives and gave it,
But no longer now the bewildering minute
Seems an absolute with eternity in it,
I did keep to sex, but interpreted,
Not all but incident the double bed,
The good communion, the shared silence,
Steps on the way to further gnosis.
Adultery was gone forever,
Instead the gold ring on your finger.

The joy of the moment poems give and gave it
But in quiet of seeking, not vinous and chanted
By the manic maidens. I am not haunted
By the Dionysian.
I seek this May morning when I should be sleeping
With whom the tryst I must be seeking.
The ways I go, what I laboured with
Must build a ship to weather death.
Aquarius, although born a fish,
Please grant me wisdom before the ash
Stains the water and I occur
Though close as breathing no longer here.

Winter Solstice (1)

How cold this winter is
And we are not yet half through it,
Perhaps it is the bias
Of this summer's unusual heat.
One is contracted to
A numbed and frozen body
And fabric the wind whistles through
As if it meant to study
Man's bare anatomy.
Bread for the winter birds
But from none of them a sweet cry;
They will be silent, those bards,
Till spring's epiphany.
The cold is an image of death
But so is the coming spring
The hedgerows quickening with
Greenery and bird song.

Winter Solstice (2)

By reaching down and putting into words
What I find there where the confusions are
I hope my explorations speak to another
Who also was dealt a wicked hand of cards.
At least that's one of the reasons why the poems get said
And to touch the heart one must have melody.
At a college I read a poem called 'Felo da Se'
And later met a girl who wanted to be dead
And maybe felt it seems this man's been there
And in his way I think come out of it,
Perhaps it's possible not to gulp barbiturate;
My poems suggest, I hope, that I do care,
Because one tries to speak to the inward ear
And exorcise with one another's fear.

Mind you that's only one reason for my writing;
I'm not a very altruistic sort of man
And really want the words to rhyme and have rhythm
Because it's no chore and most exciting.
Deprived of poetry what would I do,
Write prose, read books, drink beer and copulate?
So much joy there is though in staying up all night
Questioning silence till it answers you
And if you're lucky in words that ring quite true
And then the technique is making them ring right.
Style is getting the words accord for eternity
Cutting the rubbish out and having no clemency.

But of course one is so very much alone
If one stays human, and the syllables
Of chit-chat but confirm our separate hells;
The poems burrow down into deep joy and pain
And doing so fracture the solitude.
He or she's been down there and my deepest vision seen, –
The terrible, the beautiful, the obscene,
My sense of damnation and beatitude,
And so fractured the small circle of ego,
At least I like to think it may be so.

And whether we like it or not one can be sure
Death's coming to us either soon or late.
Do you think with dying we disintegrate?
I'll sign poems there with my proper signature
And if you ask me how the hell I know,
It's because I've been there as a human entity,
Not that I expect you to believe in me,
But I do know I've been where I'm going to go
And that with Blake, than whom no man went further,
It's just a question of passing from one room to another.

Revenants

The wind has died down now
And the house is silent,
It will be quiet tomorrow,
At least the forecasters say it.
I sit in my chair by the fire
With my wife asleep overhead
And brood upon sweetness, horror,
Not wanting to go to bed.
For the sick and the old such care,
Then napalm, and the living and dead
Pulverized by a hand's pressure;
No one has interpreted
This duality of behaviour,
That is as old as we are.

Older age brings some stiffness,
But I seem as well as ever,
Is it being human this sadness,
That will not let me alone?
About dying what should I care?
I have seen through meat, skeleton,
To continuance everywhere,
Sign by undeniable sign.

Two o'clock: in the sixth hour
Day will be here again
With all its mechanics, its stir,
That we being human sustain,
And, if not enjoy, must bear.
I hope that soon good sleep
Will take me upon its river,
And regret the black coffee I've drunk,

Though common sense will never
Sustain what I feel, what I think,
Though for thirty-two years I have been,
And with some success, some venture,
Welded into a teaching routine.

Do we regret growing old?
It is native to every creature.
One must interpret how it is spelled
Untrammelled by custom's nurture.
Is it not why we are born?
I hope in some quite soon future
To look forward to a return;
Undying, imperdurable nature.

Morituri

Such beatitudes of water
Where the scree falls to the sand
In the August sun they glitter
One might think world without end,
But tomorrow the sun may be dark and
The waters running with foam,
But it's all a grace and a Godsend
And the exile's going home.

Blake said the vegetable copy
Of eternity this world is,
There humans and flowers and the oak-tree
Shall shine with intensities,
This mundane shell the five senses
Curtails. In death sensuality
Shall enlarge and distances
And nearnesses we shall see
As they really are if the stress
Is endured; we are born to suffer,
So blessed we learn to bless.

Posthumous

I have been before my birth and after my dying
But still I am reluctant to leave being here.
Why I wonder when before and after were so clear
Should there be this strange dread of forsaking?
It is as if a bird, its cage at last open,
Should dread to leave its few imprisoned feet
The wide reaches of eternity to meet,
The thin curtain of wire at last broken.
We are accustomed to the body and this world
And fear to be at last free and unfurled.

But still it is a bore when you cannot sleep,
The ticking clock slowly eating up the hours
As first light slowly replaces the moon and stars,
A tryst with oblivion that you cannot keep.
So farewell to the kingdom of material
And let us be more alive and acutely as the dead letters spell
And growing further and at last being, well
Delivered from the five obliterating senses
And the constriction of the various tenses.

All being as it is a single moment
In which we grow and the new growth
Is the meaning in the landscape of death
And spent in heaven and heaven sent.
What matters really is the eternal
And there, there is no let or impediment.
I wonder why we are so frightened at having to die,
I shan't be sorry when I say goodbye
And have my final farthing truly spent,
I mean to the world having paid my fee
So that with no glass darkly I really see.

As I Am Known

The dawn is not golden but still it's the dawn,
Imperdurable in its forever coming on
Over the horizon's tepid line;
The hours of last night were what I worked upon,
Guiding silence out of itself into syllables
Of saying, maybe novelty, like the new day;
It's like making cryptic runes, and it tells
Of what might not have existed in the same way
If I had not worried out words from their sea bed.
It's dying that I would direct them to;
Last night I felt like choking and could hardly breathe,
Today it seems to be only a passing through
Into a communion and feeling irrelevant as the word death,
And which if I learn to live and rightly suffer
It will be more vivid than this half-life here,
At least I think so today though last night I could but offer
A variety of synonyms for fear,
The air closing in the lungs growing solid
And sodden. Now I believe death is an atmosphere
Of deeper broader reaches and not an ending.
I think of the Alps, the Dolomites,
After midnight lightning has detailed their bronze stone,
And every boulder and grass blade is saturated with light;
And that I shall know even as also I am known.

Venite

Silence is what the noises are for
As a brightness pinpoints the particular
Lightening of the sky we call a star.

It is both ordinary and peculiar
This brevity of being now and here
Where the changes occur.

There being so much objective to change by,
Not that one likes being confined in a body
But to be free of the reaches of death it is a necessity.

Ineffable are the stretches of the eternal.
Of being otherwhere and otherwise they foretell
As they approximate by slow footfall.

Nothing now is indifferent to me
Growing into becoming inevitably,
No glass, no more darkly.

See, see. Each hour nearer
To freedom, the constant wayfarer.
Do the changes continue forever?

A pause. How strange becoming is
Forever farewelling from what was,
Passing histories.

Logos

And it will come, yes, come it will,
Whether through cancer or the heart
Or old and ill, the journey start
To world's end and the other part,
Living called dying, one will be leaving
The other to get on with the grieving.
I hope for my part it will be I
Go last since pensions falter when people die
But find it hard to think of you as a finite entity,
The rift in space through which you'd be gone
And having to live outward and alone,
On the other hand I find it hard
Thinking of you living on and in want,
So let me live a bit longer
After you've gone and I'll follow
To the place where time and space are the same species
Sloughed off the transitions of the ego
So that only the self will continue
And I am more than glad to let the ego go,
The thing is a trouble and rings hollow,
Being remote from the far horizon
Where communion is God indeed,
'In the beginning was the word.'

In Memoriam: Kevin

He died from a lethal car
Mounting the pavement and smashing his head,
That small boy in his glory and power,
And is numbered among the dead.
Cancer, accident, leukaemia,
I can't understand what is meant
By a God who's omnipotent.

When the prowlers are on the rampage;
Was he drunk mounting the pavement like that?
And what will be the next stage
Of that boy whose book was shut
When only six pages were read?
Is it another birth he'll be at
Or continue to grow now he's dead?
The bough ripped off, the leaves shed.

But it's certain he'll be somewhere
In his attitude of spring,
Only not with those who are here
In their steadfast lamenting
For the shattered tree;
Is it change or necessity?

Perhaps not, perhaps, I am sure
He is with the immortals now
Though the scheme of things won't allow
Him to say where he is, where they are
And so their agony.

But the bough ripped off the tree;
The man who did it will suffer,
What does suffering not offer?
That boy dying in greenery.
On Sundays he delivered our milk
Rinsed with gaiety,
Now with the eternals he'll be
No longer as white as chalk
But blooming and beautiful.
This I believe though small
For whom death is absence, a thought,
Who only are able to see
Fading leaves, a box, a dead tree.

Rain After Drought
(Maundy Thursday)

Tonight is raining fast,
Tomorrow will surely bring
Water to a great furled flower
Too dry for blossoming,
And it will fume in summer
With its bitter fragrancy,
Nor ever again shall it wither
Since death is just something to say;
Fruit itself it will in the autumn
In which you and I are at home.

Growing Pains

Why, when there's so much that breeds about me,
A wife whom I love, daughter too, house, garden,
And a Snowdon cottage for us by the mountains and near the sea,
Books, quite a number of which I've written,
Am I stalked by this misery?

Surely what one has and does does matter
And for thirty years I've trafficked with
What should I say, students and children
Increasing the nervous shoots of life
By the knowledge I have garnered
From joy and grief and the hours alone
Shaping poems which some say do offer
Of truth a thin but meaningful life-line.
But still this animal of anguish
Stalks me whether I am asleep or awake,
Whatever subterfuge I use to banish,
It's ever, always species of heartbreak.

It's the dead time now and the sun's
Shortest span and of growth the nadir;
Latent till some warmth again begins,
Aconite and snowdrop wait for better weather,
Sunshine and the coming up of the New Year.
My last term is soon starting as a teacher
And soon on my own without a routine
I shall concentrate on being a writer,
Freed from most of the living and earning machine.
From the bad saliva so tart and bitter
On my tongue, and in my veins
From the shoots of greenish poison, heart of my hearts deliver;
May I continue to grow but with less of the growing pains.

Speed, Speed

It is now the second night
I have been unable to sleep,
Wakeful I hear the lap
Of darkness breaking on shores,
Of trees and city squares,
Expecting bird song and first light
To fuse over the rinsed scars.
I have walked in my working room
From typewriter to chairs,
And with certainty they came,
Rhythmic, a form of words,
Driven, crested with foam,
To my stained, sea-shaken hand
Tapping the keys in a room.
Very soon I will understand
This symmetrical energy
And why it has come to me
Typing in the thinning dark;
Sixty-one and so much unsaid;
Speed, speed, to work, to work;
The first light is coloured red.

Gerard Manley Hopkins

Hyperaesthesia was his faithful wife
And he could see the stress and the inscape
Of swivelling water and of wimpling wind
And the unchristened horror of the ape.
Into some aspects of phenomena
No one saw further than this Jesuit priest,
But he wrenched his vision of things as they are
To piebald images of Jesus Christ
And so did violence to a metaphor.
For the Windhover, Oxford, Inversnaid,
Could never be illustrations of dogma,
Only themselves. It seems he was afraid
Of letting creatures be just as they are.
Tying his vision to some clinching moral,
Within himself he almost choked dear life
And the outcome of this insidious quarrel
Might well have been some bland Victorian hymn.
But hyperaesthesia was his faithful wife
And selved him into novel ways of seeing,
He pruned stale nature with a verbal knife
To expose the scape and stress of green leaves growing.
And then there came his terrible Dies Irae
And cries, cries, countless, like dead letters sent
To dearest him who lives alas away.
It's hard to know just what is really meant;
But I suspect for this man, poet and priest,
Is just what made the sacred cauldron bubble.
But when he came at forty-six to die
And said three times, 'I am so very happy.'
Was it oblivion that nerved his tongue,
Or an image of Christ, the bluebell and the lily?

OHIO UNIVERSITY LIBRARY

Please return this book as soon as you have finished with it. In order to avoid a fine it must be returned by the latest date stamped below.

CF